LIGHTNING BOLT BOOKS™

Dwarf Rabbits

Buffy Silverman

Lerner Publications • Minneapolis

Lerner Publications Company
A division of Lerner Publishing Group, Inc.
241 First Avenue North
Minneapolis, MN 55401 USA

For reading levels and more information, look up this title at www.lernerbooks.com.

Library of Congress Cataloging-in-Publication Data

The Cataloging-in-Publication Data for *Dwarf Rabbits* is on file at the Library of Congress.
ISBN 978-1-5415-1029-6 (lib. bdg.)
ISBN 978-1-5415-1186-6 (pbk.)
ISBN 978-1-5415-1030-2 (EB pdf)

Manufactured in the United States of America
1-43955-33970-6/19/2017

Table of Contents

Meet the Dwarf Rabbit

A tiny pet hops along the floor. It wiggles its nose and looks around with its large eyes. It is a dwarf rabbit!

Netherland dwarf rabbits are the most common kind of dwarf rabbit.

Dwarf rabbits are usually smaller than other kinds of rabbits. Some rabbits can be 5.5 pounds (2.5 kg). But most dwarf rabbits grow to only about 2 or 3 pounds (0.9 to 1.4 kg).

Dwarf rabbits have round bodies and large heads. Their little tails are attached to their back ends. They have thin ears on the top of their heads.

Dwarf rabbits come in many different colors. Their hair can be white, black, brown, gray, orange, or yellow.

This dwarf lop rabbit has gray and white fur.

A Dwarf Rabbit Is Born

A dwarf rabbit is getting ready to have babies. She climbs into a wooden nest box. She adds some of her hair to the nest. Then she gives birth to her babies.

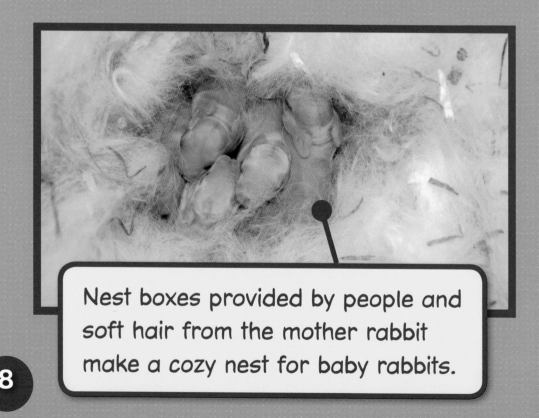

Nest boxes provided by people and soft hair from the mother rabbit make a cozy nest for baby rabbits.

Tiny dwarf rabbits are born with their eyes shut. They have no hair. A person carefully puts a baby in the nest if it is born out of the box.

Baby rabbits are called kits. Their mother is a doe.

Newborn kits drink their mother's milk. The doe nurses her kits once a day. In ten days, the kits will open their eyes.

People should begin to hold the kits after they open their eyes. This will help the rabbits get used to humans.

Young kits hop and play. People adopt kits that are at least eight weeks old.

The kits start to eat hay and feed when they are three weeks old. They will be ready to leave their mother when they are six weeks old.

Dwarf Rabbit Life

Dwarf rabbits can live inside your home. They sleep and eat inside a cage. But they need time playing outside of their cages too.

It might take some time before a dwarf rabbit feels safe in a new home.

Dwarf rabbits are small and can get hurt if people don't handle them carefully. Be gentle when holding or petting a dwarf rabbit.

Rabbits explore their homes. Sit on the floor, and let a dwarf rabbit get to know you. It sniffs and rubs against people. It chews rabbit toys and digs and climbs.

Rabbits are most active in the morning and evening. They run and jump with their strong legs.

Make sure a rabbit's play space is safe. Clear away all cords and other items that could be dangerous for rabbits to chew.

Caring for A Dwarf Rabbit

Dwarf rabbits can learn their names. They can learn to use a litter box. They can even learn to jump onto your lap!

A water bottle hangs from a rabbit's cage. The rabbit needs fresh water, feed, and hay every day. Its cage needs to be cleaned at least once a week.

Rabbits eat both hay and feed.

A rabbit's teeth are always growing. It chews on rabbit toys to wear them down. Sometimes the teeth get too long. A vet can trim a rabbit's front teeth and nails.

A rabbit sits quietly to have its hair brushed. It might lick your hands. **That is a dwarf rabbit's way of saying that you are part of its family!**

Dwarf Rabbit Diagram

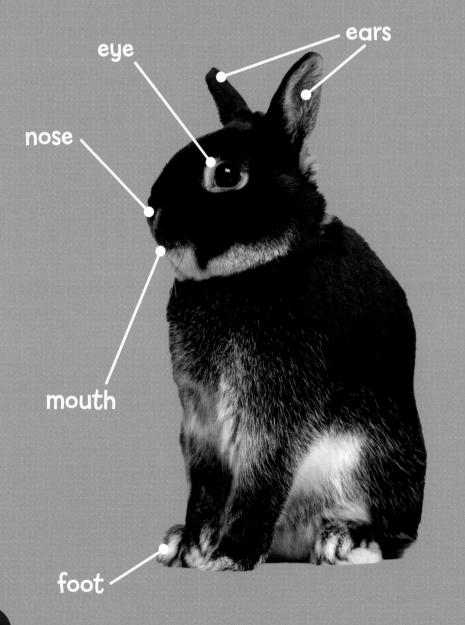

eye

ears

nose

mouth

foot

Fun Facts

- Rabbits may eat their own poop! Some rabbit poop has special nutrition in it. Rabbits eat this poop to stay healthy.

- Rabbits make many different sounds. They squeal when they are scared. They click their teeth when they are happy. If a rabbit grunts or growls, it might be ready to bite.

- Wild rabbits thump their back feet against the ground to warn other rabbits of danger. A pet rabbit might do this to warn its people too!

Glossary

doe: a female rabbit

feed: special food for a rabbit

kit: a baby rabbit

litter box: a container that is used as a toilet by a rabbit or other pet

nest box: a box in which a rabbit makes a nest for her young

newborn: an animal or person that was recently born

nurse: to feed milk from a mother's body to a baby

vet: a doctor who cares for animals. *Vet* is short for *veterinarian*.

Further Reading

Boothroyd, Jennifer. *Meet a Baby Rabbit.* Minneapolis: Lerner Publications, 2017.

National Geographic: Amazing Animals
http://kids.nationalgeographic.com/explore
/adventure_pass/amazing-animals/quacky
-friendship/

Newman, Aline Alexander. *Rascally Rabbits! And More True Stories of Animals Behaving Badly!* Washington, DC: National Geographic, 2016.

"Pets 101—Rabbits"
https://www.youtube.com/watch?v=pzSRFpa5CPc

Science Kids: Fun Rabbit Facts for Kids
http://www.sciencekids.co.nz/sciencefacts/animals
/rabbit.html

Silverman, Buffy. *Pygmy Goats.* Minneapolis: Lerner Publications, 2018.

Index

Photo Acknowledgments

The images in this book are used with the permission of: iStock.com/ksena32, p. 2; Soultkd/ Shutterstock.com, pp. 4, 11; Bildagentur Zoonar GmbH/Shutterstock.com, p. 5; Grigorita Ko/ Shutterstock.com, p. 6; zandyz/Shutterstock.com, p. 7; © Scay21/Dreamstime.com, p. 8; Arco Images GmbH/Alamy Stock Photo, p. 9; Pressmaster/Shutterstock.com, p. 10; poyja/ Shutterstock.com, p. 12; iStock.com/SurkovDimitri, p. 13; © Mark Eastment/Dreamstime.com, p. 14; © danny gormley/Dreamstime.com, p. 15; iStock.com/zocchi2, p. 16; Francesco83/ Shutterstock.com, p. 17; bmf-foto.de/Shutterstock.com, p. 18; imageBROKER/Alamy Stock Photo, p. 19; iStock.com/GlobalP, p. 20; Eric Isselee/Shutterstock.com, p. 22.

Front cover: May_Chanikran/Shutterstock.com.

Main body text set in Billy Infant regular 28/36. Typeface provided by SparkType.